HEINEMANN
Profiles

Nelson Mandela

An Unauthorized Biography

Sean Connolly

Heinemann Library
Chicago, Illinois

Designed by Visual Image
Originated by Dot Gradations
Printed in Hong Kong

05 04 03 02 01
10 9 8 7 6 5 4 3 2 1

Library of Congress Cataloging-in-Publication Data

Connolly, Sean, 1956-
        Nelson Mandela / Sean Connolly.
            p. cm. – (Heinemann profiles)
        Includes bibliographical references and index.
        Summary: A biography of the South African leader, discussing his childhood, family
    life, career, imprisonment, and election as president.
        ISBN 1-57572-225-9 (lib. binding)
        1. Mandela, Nelson, 1918---Juvenile literature. 2. Presidents—South
    Africa—Biography—Juvenile literature. [1. Mandela, Nelson, 1918- 2. Presidents—South
    Africa. 3. Civil rights workers. 4. Blacks—South Africa—Biography.] I. Title. II. Series.

DT1949.M35 C65 2000
968.06'5—dc21
                                                                    99-085742

Acknowledgments
The Publishers would like to thank the following for permission to reproduce photographs: Associated Press, p. 30; Associated Press/J.-M. Bouju, p. 47; Bailey's African History Archives, pp. 22, 27; Bailey's African History Archives/Drum, pp. 14, 16, 26; Bailey's African History Archives/A. Kumalo, p. 31; Bailey's African History Archives/Peter Magubane, pp. 4, 28; Bailey's African History Archives/Jurgen Schadeberg, pp. 20, 24; Penni Bickle, p. 33; Corbis-Bettmann/UPI, p. 8; Mayibuye Centre, pp. 7, 13, 19, 34; Popperfoto/Reuters, p. 39; Rex Features, pp. 10, 25, 29, 40, 42, 44, 45, 46, 48, 49, 50; Rex Features/Nils Jorgensen, p. 37; Rex Features/M. Zeffler, p. 43.

Cover photograph reproduced with permission of Rex Features.

Every effort has been made to contact copyright holders of any material reproduced in this book. Any omissions will be rectified in subsequent printings if notice is given to the Publisher.

Some words are shown in bold, **like this.** You can find out what they mean by looking in the Glossary.

This is an unauthorized biography. The subject has not sponsored or endorsed this book.

CONTENTS

WHO IS NELSON MANDELA?

Nelson Mandela has always faced the future with optimism and confidence.

As the twentieth century drew to a close, many people looked back at the last hundred years to try to make sense of all the changes that took place. There were two terrible world wars—in which millions of people died—as well as further wars and conflicts, some of which continue to this day. To some observers, it seems as though there is no way in which hatred and injustice can be defeated.

SHINING EXAMPLE

Other people take a more hopeful view, looking at the work of brave individuals who have suffered greatly in order to promote peace and equality. Nelson Mandela is one such individual. Born in a country in which the majority of the population was denied basic **human rights,** he nevertheless managed to educate himself and become a leading figure in the efforts to improve life in South Africa. In the end, he did succeed in improving life for the people of his country.

Along the way, Mandela suffered even more than his countrymen from the harsh political system in South Africa. The cruel system of **apartheid** made it almost impossible for non-whites to find good housing, work, or even the means to travel within their own country. In addition to this, his efforts to promote change led to nearly 30 years in prison.

EXTENDING A HAND

Nelson Mandela's long period in prison only strengthened his will to improve life in his country. The world gradually became aware of his struggle and offered support to his cause. Nelson Mandela waited patiently until a South African leader arrived who was prepared to listen to the international community, and who was willing to release him.

Without sacrificing any of his ideals, Nelson Mandela emerged from prison and was able almost immediately to change the face of South Africa. Again, the world welcomed his efforts. He never claimed to be a saint, just a man who was determined to make his country a better place for everyone living there. Even as leader of South Africa, he met difficulties, but he led the country by his own example of courage, decency, and fairness. For these simple virtues, tested by the harshest opposition, he remains an example for the whole world.

A RURAL CHILDHOOD

Nelson Mandela was born on July 18, 1918, in a tiny village called Mvezo in the region of South Africa known as Transkei. This area is rich farming country, with rolling hills, fertile soil, and many rivers to keep the land well-watered. Most people in Transkei lived—and still live today—in small villages like Mvezo. The most important person in the village is the chief, who makes many decisions and settles disputes among villagers.

A ROYAL CONNECTION

Nelson's father, Gadla Henry Mphakanyiswa Mandela, was the chief in Mvezo. He also had another important connection, with the royal family of the Thembu people who lived in that part of Transkei. Nelson's father, like his father before him, was trained to give advice to the Thembu kings. Part of this role was to record the history of the Thembu people, as well as the larger Xhosa nation of which they are a part.

It is common for Thembu chiefs to have more than one wife. Nelson's mother, Nosekeni Fanny, was the third of the chief's four wives. All together, the chief had four sons and nine daughters. The youngest boy, who grew to become the famous Nelson Mandela, was named Rolihlahla, which means "pulling the branch of the tree" in the Xhosa language, but more commonly means "troublemaker" or "stirring up trouble." He was given the name Nelson by a teacher when he began school. She thought that black children would get along better in life if the British rulers could recognize and pronounce their names, so she chose English names for them. Mandela may have been named for Admiral Horatio Nelson, a British hero.

Traditional houses in Transkei were built to reflect the intense heat of the South African sun.

UPROOTED

The British ruled South Africa when Nelson was a child. They accepted some of the tribal divisions among black South Africans because the divisions made the country as a whole easier to rule. The Thembu were one of many such groupings of black South Africans. When Nelson was a baby, his father, a proud man, had a disagreement with a local British official and lost his position. Nelson and three of his sisters had to leave Mvezo with their

The great Indian leader Mohandas Gandhi trained as a lawyer in South Africa in order to fight injustice. Nelson's early career would take the same path.

mother and move to another village, Qunu, where Nelson spent most of his childhood. Nelson's mother's family helped to support her and her children. They had little money, but Nelson and the other village boys were free to play in the **veld** and to look after the villagers' sheep and cattle.

At home in the evenings, Nelson's mother would tell the children about the history and legends of the Xhosa people. These stories made a great impression on the young boy, and he became very proud of his nation's history.

South Africa in the 1920s

South Africa was controlled by the British in the 1920s. The British had gained full control over South Africa after defeating the **Afrikaners** in the Boer War, which ended in 1902. Britain united the different parts of South Africa with the Act of Union of 1910. At the same time, it offered limited freedom of government to some of the parts of South Africa which were previously ruled by the Afrikaners. The Afrikaners, like the British, were white. The position for non-white South Africans—and in particular for black South Africans—was very different. In some parts of South Africa, a tiny minority of blacks and **coloreds** could vote, but real power lay with the white rulers. Black South Africans were able to look after some of their affairs locally, as in the Thembu Court of Justice, but the black population had no real say in how the country itself was run.

A GLIMPSE OF POWER

When Nelson was nine years old, his father came to Qunu to visit that branch of his large family. He was very tired and was suffering from a serious lung disease. After several days of rest in one of the family's huts, Nelson's father died. Nelson and his family were very sad, but his mother also had a new problem—how to bring up her children without any income.

THE ROYAL HOUSEHOLD

Nelson's family connection with the royal family of Thembuland came to the rescue. Chief Jongintaba Dalindyebo, the **regent** of the royal family, offered to act as Nelson's **guardian.** The chief considered Nelson to be, in effect, part of his extended family. Nelson had to leave the village and his friends to move to the regent's home in Mqhekezweni, the capital of Thembuland. Nelson's mother went with him to the new home, but then had to return to her other children in Qunu after a few days.

As a teenager, Nelson Mandela enjoyed many benefits of his family's royal connections.

Life in the new home was very different from anything Nelson had seen before. He saw cars and electric lights, as well as far more white people. One of the regent's responsibilities was to settle disputes, much as Nelson's own father had done, but on a larger scale. In this role, the regent **presided** over the Thembu Court of Justice. Nelson would watch and listen as the court heard cases. He was very interested in doing what was fair and right, and he decided to become a lawyer. In the large house, he also listened to the conversations of the **elders** of the Thembu people. They spoke of the many wars that their **ancestors** had fought in defense of their lands. Nelson enjoyed hearing and learning from these stories, and he began to consider his people's struggle for freedom.

A GOOD EDUCATION

The regent insisted that Nelson should have all of the advantages that his own children enjoyed. One of these was a good education, so Nelson was sent to Clarkebury Boarding Institute when he was sixteen years old. He studied hard at this school, and made friends with the other young Thembu boys and girls there. In 1937, when he was nineteen, Nelson enrolled at Healdtown, which was similar to an American high school. Very few black people had this opportunity, but Nelson had the advantage of belonging to a wealthy, well-connected family.

> "For too long we have succumbed to the false gods of the white man. But we shall emerge and cast off these foreign notions."
>
> Xhosa poet Krune Mqhayi, addressing Healdtown students

Nelson had a difficult schedule at Healdtown, but the discipline he learned there served him well later in life. Students awoke at six in the morning and began a long day's work, with only skimpy meals to break up the studies, which would last until five. There would be more studying in the evening until lights went out at 9:30 P.M.

One day, near the end of Nelson's stay at Healdtown, the students were addressed by a famous Xhosa poet, Krune Mqhayi. Nelson was startled to hear Mqhayi's words. Speaking in Xhosa, the poet made a powerful prediction—that one day, black Africans would rule themselves. The words were dramatic, and Nelson took them as a personal challenge.

LIFELONG FRIENDS

Obeying the **regent's** wishes, Nelson enrolled at the University College of Fort Hare in 1938. This establishment was the only place of higher learning for black Africans at that time. If he graduated, Nelson would become the first member of the regent's **clan** to obtain a college degree. Fort Hare had been founded as a **missionary** college, and it still insisted on Christian behavior from its students. However, it was also a center for proud young

Africans to learn more about their own culture and history. Many of the teachers agreed with the words Nelson had heard from Mqhayi, and the students constantly debated the African struggle among themselves. Many of them hoped that the black **majority** would one day come to rule the country.

One of the friends Nelson made in these discussions was a serious science student named Oliver Tambo. This new friend was a good debater, and he always listened to what the others said before opening his mouth. The two young men spent a lot of time together, attending church services as well as the lively student debates.

Oliver Tambo became Nelson's lifelong friend and ally in South Africa's struggle for freedom.

Nelson was also gaining a reputation as a quick thinker and good speaker. He was elected to the Student Representative Council (SRC), but this new position soon landed him in trouble. The SRC insisted on better food at Fort Hare, and threatened a **boycott** if conditions did not improve. The authorities refused the demand, and Nelson was **expelled** from Fort Hare for his role in the protest.

LIFE IN THE CITY

Nelson was worried when he returned to Mqhekezweni. He knew that the **regent** would be furious when he learned how the young man's antics had gotten him **expelled** from Fort Hare. The regent made his position clear: Nelson must be prepared to abandon the Fort Hare **boycott** and return to school the following year. The authorities at Fort Hare had offered to accept Nelson back if he would give up his position.

Walter Sisulu convinced Nelson of the need to continue with his studies.

A FORCED HAND

Back at Mqhekezweni, Nelson resumed his normal activities, helping the regent and watching as cases were tried. He was pleased when the regent's son, named Justice, joined him. The two young men had become close friends during Nelson's years at Mqhekezweni, and they looked forward to more good times. But then the pair of them had some upsetting news: the regent was planning a marriage for each of the young men. This was devastating, since neither young man really knew the young woman that he was meant to marry. It also seemed to spell the end of their independence.

Both Nelson and Justice knew that the regent would not agree if the young men asked to remain unmarried for the time being. He was simply doing what was expected of him—making sure that the **clan** continued into the next generation. In 1940, Nelson and Justice decided that their only choice was to run away and start a new life.

THE BIG CITY

Nelson and Justice made their way by train to South Africa's largest city, Johannesburg. They had the passes required by the police, but they needed other documents, such as a letter from a boss or **guardian,** once they arrived in the city. After some difficulties along the way, they finally found jobs at Crown Mines, the largest gold mine in Johannesburg. Within a day, though, the boys' new boss found out that they had run away, and he fired them.

Now they were alone in the big city with no jobs and no money. Nelson and Justice decided to try to find work separately and to meet again in the George Goch **township,** where a cousin of Nelson's lived. The cousin was impressed by Nelson, and helped him meet influential people.

One of these people was a successful young businessman named Walter Sisulu. Nelson was encouraged by meeting a fellow black man who seemed confident in the world of Johannesburg. Walter advised Nelson to continue his education and fulfill his dream of becoming a lawyer. Nelson could do this by taking a **correspondence course,** but in the meantime, Nelson needed a job.

LEARNING THE LAW

Walter also found work for Nelson, with the legal firm of Witkin, Sidelsky and Eidelman. One of the partners in this firm, Lazar Sidelsky, was a friend of Walter's, and was eager to promote the education and training of young black lawyers. Sidelsky agreed to take Nelson on as an **articled clerk,** providing Nelson with an income and a chance to see law in action. In the evenings, Nelson studied law by correspondence with the University of South Africa in order to earn the degree that he needed to become a lawyer.

The law firm was the perfect place for Nelson to meet white people who were kind and who had no **prejudice** against black South Africans. By making friends with others who worked there, he met people from the various **ethnic** backgrounds that make up South Africa—not just blacks and whites, but Indians and **coloreds.** At night, though, Nelson had to return to Alexandra, one of the townships where blacks lived. Alexandra had no electricity, and there was a great deal of crime, but most of the people did their best to help each other out.

Pass laws

For many years, it was difficult for black South Africans to travel within their country. The government insisted that each black person, known as an "African" (as opposed to a white person), carry a special pass. This document was like a passport, except that people needed to show them to white policemen inside their own country whenever they were asked. The pass acted as a way of controlling where black people lived and worked. A person could be arrested or even put in prison for failing to produce a pass.

Joining the Movement

Nelson was still working for the law firm in Johannesburg and studying at night when he learned in 1942 that the **regent** had died. Nelson and his former **guardian** had had several disagreements about Nelson's independent spirit, but the death of the older man made Nelson very sad. He returned to Mqhekezweni for the funeral, and found he was teased for the way his Xhosa pronunciation had changed. In the relatively short time he had lived in Johannesburg, Nelson had acquired a slight Zulu accent. Rather than feel ashamed by this, Nelson simply felt that the change in his speech reflected the way in which he now felt closer to all South Africans, regardless of their background. After the funeral, Justice stayed behind to act as regent, but Nelson returned to the big city to pursue his own plans.

Part of the Struggle

Later in 1942, Nelson passed the final examination for his college degree. He also became more friendly with a fellow worker named Gaur Radebe, who spoke at length of the need for black Africans to improve their own conditions. Gaur took Nelson along to meetings of the African National Congress (ANC), where Nelson saw passionate debates about subjects ranging from racial equality to bus fares.

After attending several meetings, Nelson realized that Walter Sisulu was one of the leaders in the organization. Nelson began spending much of his free time at Walter's house in the Orlando district. Discussions continued long into the night, often accompanied by huge meals cooked by Walter's mother. Nelson became a member of the ANC, and became well-known in the local area for his intelligence and dedication. There were also other familiar faces joining Nelson at these meetings, including his old friend Oliver Tambo.

Nelson married trainee nurse Evelyn Mase after meeting her at Walter Sisulu's house.

ATTRACTING THE YOUNG

One of the ANC members that Nelson and Oliver met at Walter's house was a young lawyer named Anton Lembede. He was one of the few black lawyers in South Africa, so Nelson paid special attention to what he said. Lembede was a forceful speaker who complained that the ANC was stuck in the past. In his view, the ANC leadership was too timid and approached the struggle for black independence in the wrong way. Instead of sending polite **petitions** to the white government and acting strictly within the unfair rules set out by the government, he wanted the ANC to be more **aggressive.** The movement needed to show the government that it represented the vast **majority** of South Africans, and not just a core of well-educated black people in the cities.

Nelson took pride in his neat appearance. He knew that he was an example for other young African leaders.

Nelson and Oliver Tambo agreed with Lembede's views about the ANC and the need for change. Like him, they wanted the struggle for freedom to be more of a **grass-roots** movement, appealing to people living in the countryside as well as those living in the cities. In particular, the ANC needed to attract younger members. With this goal in mind, Nelson Mandela, Oliver Tambo, Walter Sisulu, and about 60 other ANC members decided to form a youth branch of the ANC. They worked within the organization to do this, and on Easter Sunday 1944, in a social center in Johannesburg, they officially launched the ANC Youth League (ANCYL).

The African National Congress

The African National Congress (ANC) was formed in 1912 as a way of improving the living conditions of the black majority in South Africa. It was the oldest national African organization in the country, and it tried to attract members from the many tribal groups that make up South Africa. At the time the ANC was founded, and for many years afterwards, blacks could not vote, own land, or travel freely in their own country. The goal of the ANC was to make black people full citizens of South Africa. However, unlike groups with similar goals in other African countries, the ANC wanted the change to come from within the existing system. The ANC **constitution** banned **radical** activities and violence, and concentrated instead on stating its requests with polite dignity.

A RISING STAR

Nelson Mandela impressed his fellow ANC members with his discipline and determination. He was elected to the **secretaryship** of the ANCYL in 1947. Along with Walter Sisulu, Oliver Tambo, and other young ANC members, Mandela promoted the idea of change within the movement.

INTERNAL BATTLES

Not everyone was pleased with the changing attitude of young ANC members. In particular, Dr. A. B. Xuma, head of the ANC, felt that things were changing too fast. Dr. Xuma was well-respected within the ANC because he had helped the organization grow and gain more money. But in Nelson's view, Dr. Xuma had become too "English." The doctor had many friends and contacts within the white **establishment,** and he felt that disagreements could be resolved quietly, as they would be between English gentlemen.

This clash of ideas became more apparent after the general election of 1948. As in other South African elections, only whites could vote.

Afrikaner Nationalist Dr. D. F. Malan addresses a large crowd of supporters.

The Program of Action

The Program of Action was one of many important documents that Nelson Mandela helped write for the ANC. It set specific goals for the ANC in the fight against injustice. The main demands were that all South Africans have equal rights as citizens, in education, **parliamentary representation**, property ownership, and work. And unlike most previous ANC documents, it presented its goals as a series of demands rather than requests. Mandela and other leading ANC members spoke at illegal meetings around the country, explaining the ANC position to fellow blacks, and building **grass-roots** support.

The new government, under the National Party, formed a harsh new system of laws known as **apartheid.** The previous system of mostly unofficial restrictions against blacks was bad enough, but the new apartheid laws made life even harder for the non-white **majority.** Young ANC members felt that they must be more forceful in their defiance of the new laws, so they drew up a Program of Action.

The program, which Mandela, Oliver Tambo, and Walter Sisulu helped to write, called for the ANC to use the weapons of **strikes, boycotts,** and **civil disobedience.** The program became official ANC policy in 1949, when Dr. J. S. Moroka replaced the **conservative** Dr. Xuma as ANC president. Younger men began to replace older members throughout the ANC, and in 1950, Nelson Mandela was elected to the National Executive Committee (NEC) of the ANC.

THE STRUGGLE CONTINUES

With its dynamic new leadership, the ANC continued to press its case for equality within South Africa. In 1952, it launched its Campaign for the Defiance of Unjust Laws. Again, Mandela played an important role, this time as national volunteer-in-chief. This post meant that Mandela traveled around South Africa persuading ordinary people to not to obey the harsh **apartheid** laws. For their part in this campaign, Mandela and others with him were arrested under the Suppression of Communism Act. The judge, whom Mandela respected, agreed that the men had not encouraged people to use violence, so they got only a **suspended sentence** of two years. This sentence meant, however, that Mandela was not allowed to attend gatherings or to leave Johannesburg.

The law office of Mandela and Tambo was the first black legal practice in Johannesburg.

LEGAL ACTION

Mandela put his time to good use, and finally became qualified to practice law. In 1952, Mandela and Oliver Tambo opened their own legal office in Johannesburg. The two lawyers tried to help their clients—most of whom were also non-whites—in their struggle against the apartheid laws. Mandela continued to use his knowledge of the law throughout his life.

At the 1952 annual conference of the ANC, Chief Albert Luthuli was elected president, replacing Dr. Moroka. Although he was not allowed to attend, Nelson Mandela was appointed first deputy president. Mandela took his responsibilities seriously, and campaigned for better education and living conditions for all South Africans. At the same time, he continued to practice law.

In June 1958 Nelson Mandela married his second wife, Winnie Nomzamo Madikizela. He and his first wife, Evelyn, had divorced because she did not agree with his deep involvement with the ANC.

In late 1957, Mandela was charged again, this time with **treason**. He was one of several ANC members who were singled out because of their important positions. The government claimed that the ANC leaders had been preparing to overthrow the government by violence and to replace it with a **communist** government. The trial lasted several years.

> "We had risen in professional status in our community, but every case in court, every visit to the prisons to interview clients, reminded us of the humiliation and suffering burning into our people."
>
> Oliver Tambo, recalling his legal partnership with Nelson Mandela

AN UNFOLDING DRAMA

During the late 1950s, when Mandela's **treason** trial was in progress, Africa was going through many changes. The European **colonial** powers, such as the France and the United Kingdom (U.K.), were granting independence to many former colonies.

SHARPEVILLE

At the same time, nothing was really changing in South Africa. The government was putting into practice its Bantustan policy, which forced many black South Africans to move into **homelands** approved by the government. Nelson Mandela argued forcefully against this policy, and his actions earned him several **banning orders.**

Mandela and his fellow defendants remained confident throughout their long treason trial.

By now, black South Africans had mounted several large protests against **apartheid.** In March 1960, several thousand people gathered in the **township** of Sharpeville, near Johannesburg. The 75 police present panicked, opening fire on the unarmed demonstrators. Within seconds, 69 demonstrators were dead. The reaction to

The Sharpeville tragedy forced the ANC to continue its struggle by means of force.

this tragedy echoed around the world. The South African government responded by declaring a **state of emergency** and by making the ANC illegal. From then on, the ANC had to continue its struggle **underground**.

BATTLE LINES

A rare piece of good news cheered the ANC on March 29, 1961, when the treason trial involving Nelson Mandela collapsed. Mandela participated more fully in the secret ANC plans and helped launch a new branch of the ANC. This new group, called Umkhonto we Sizwe (Spear of the Nation), but known to most people simply as MK, would be the armed core of the ANC and would prepare to continue the struggle by force. Mandela would be its chief. In effect, his task was to form an army. But although Mandela was technically free after the collapse of the treason trial, he knew that the government was waiting to arrest him again. He felt that his only chance of continuing his job was to move secretly around the country, keeping one step ahead of those who would be on his trail.

Nelson Mandela represented the ANC at the All-in Africa conference in 1961.

Mandela was breaking many **apartheid** laws in his travels around the country, and there was a **warrant** for his arrest issued almost as soon as he went on the run. The continued freedom of a well-known public figure like Nelson Mandela bothered the police, and they became more determined to stop him. With each day that passed, they increased their efforts to trap him.

THE BLACK PIMPERNEL

Mandela's main strategy was to stay in a safe hiding place during the day, and to concentrate on his work at night. The ANC and other organizations helped locate safe places for him to stay, sometimes for months at a time. Mandela also remained on the run by becoming "invisible," or trying to blend in with the people around him. He took less care with his appearance, knowing that the vast majority of black South Africans could not afford to look as clean-cut as he normally did. One of his best disguises was as a chauffeur. Any police who saw him driving his car would think that he was on an errand for his white master.

Mandela and Oliver Tambo met up in Ethiopia in 1962.

Mandela also made daring reports to the newspapers, making fun of the government in an effort to raise the spirit of the black majority. Nelson's exploits earned him the nickname "the Black Pimpernel," after the Scarlet Pimpernel—a character in a story set in the French Revolution.

FOREIGN SUPPORT

Using money that the ANC had built up over the years, Mandela was secretly taken out of South Africa to neighboring Botswana and was then able to fly to many countries, including Tanganyika (now part of Tanzania), Ghana, Liberia, and Ethiopia. In Algeria, he underwent military training. Mandela also formed personal friendships with many African leaders on this trip.

"I will not leave South Africa, nor will I surrender. Only through hardship, sacrifice, and **militant** action can freedom be won. The struggle is my life. I will continue fighting for freedom until the end of my days."

Nelson Mandela, June 26, 1961, in a letter released to newspapers while he was on the run

THE RIVONIA TRIAL

In December 1960, while Mandela was still in hiding, he received the news that Chief Luthuli of the ANC had been awarded the Nobel Peace Prize. The South African government, however, was angry that an ANC leader was so honored, and began to cause more trouble for the organization. Soon Mandela was summoned back by the ANC and flown to a secret location in South Africa.

BEHIND BARS

Mandela went to the unofficial ANC headquarters at Lilliesleaf Farm in Rivonia, not far from Johannesburg. From there, he traveled around South Africa, checking on ANC units and their plans for action. Then, on the night of August 5, 1962, he was captured by police who had followed his trail.

Chief Albert Luthuli was awarded the Nobel Peace Prize only nine months after the Sharpeville tragedy.

Charged with leaving the country illegally, Mandela was convicted and sentenced to five years in prison.

THE BIG ARREST

Mandela was already in prison when South African police discovered the secret ANC military high command at Lilliesleaf Farm. Among the documents that they found was a plan called Operation Mayibuye, a strategy for **guerrilla** warfare in South Africa. This was a serious threat to the government, and in October, Mandela and ten other **activists,** including Walter Sisulu, were charged with **sabotage.**

The trial, which soon became known as the Rivonia Trial, began in October 1963. Mandela, Sisulu, and the other defendants pleaded not guilty to the charges; they felt that the state, or government, was unfair and not based on **democratic** ideals. South Africa—and the rest of the world—waited to see how the trial would develop. If the men were found guilty, they could face the death penalty.

LIFE IN PRISON

T he state continued its case until February 29, 1964. The team of lawyers representing the **defendants** disagreed on whether the eleven should **testify.** Most of the defendants wanted to testify, partly to explain that their plans for **sabotage** were not meant to injure people. Finally, they convinced the lawyers to let them make their statements.

Mandela spoke first, describing the inequality in South African life, and noting that the ANC plans were not to promote **civil war,** but to prepare for it. Walter Sisulu and the others continued this theme. Meanwhile, people around the world held **vigils** in support of the defendants. The trial continued for months, until eventually, on June 11, 1964, Mandela and the other main defendants were all found guilty. They had to spend the night in suspense, waiting to see if they would receive the death penalty.

THE ISLAND

On June 12, Mandela and the others were sentenced to life in prison. Mandela's wife, Winnie, and his mother were both in the courtroom, but in the confusion, he never saw the looks of relief on their faces. The news was indeed a relief, but Mandela and the other convicted men still had to face an immense challenge—keeping their courage and determination in a prison system that was even harsher to blacks than to other South Africans.

As if to prove this point, the state sent the prisoners to the famous Robben Island prison, which stands several miles off Cape Town in Table Bay. A plane took the prisoners to the island, where they were met by grim guards with automatic weapons. A cold winter wind blew in from the sea, going right through their thin prison clothes. The guards did not speak to the prisoners except to deliver simple one-word commands such as "Halt," "Move," or "Silence." It became clear immediately what life in prison would be like.

It would be very difficult for any prisoners to escape from an island prison so far from shore.

STERN DISCIPLINE

The hard lessons in discipline that Mandela had learned during his schooling now worked to his advantage. Conditions were hard, and the prisoners were forced to work long hours, either sewing clothes or crushing stones into gravel. The prison authorities allowed few visits from the prisoners' wives and families, and made it almost impossible for them to find out what was happening in the outside world. Mandela could not watch his family grow, nor could he be with them to share their grief when his oldest son died in a car crash in 1969.

Nelson Mandela and Walter Sisulu kept up their close friendship during their years in prison.

In order to boost **morale** and discipline, Mandela and many other prisoners read whatever books they could find. Some prisoners even studied for degrees while behind bars; Robben Island was known as "the University" by some of the men imprisoned there. Prisoners also learned a great deal from each other, and they formed groups to meet and discuss ideas.

Mandela also found that he was continuing his legal practice, even though it was in an unusual setting. Many prisoners were trying to form **appeals** to get out of prison, but they did not have the legal knowledge to do this or the money to hire lawyers. Mandela offered his services to help prepare the necessary documents.

Nelson Mandela's words at the end of his trial in 1964 stand as one of the most dramatic statements of political ideals:

"I have fought against white domination and I have fought against black domination. I have cherished the ideal of a **democratic** and free society in which all persons live together in harmony and with equal opportunities. It is an ideal which I hope to live for and to achieve. But if needs be, it is an ideal for which I am prepared to die."

DEALING WITH THE ENEMY

Life on Robben Island was **monotonous** and dreary despite the efforts that prisoners made to keep each other active, educated, and cheerful. In many ways, the worst part of prison life was not being able to help loved ones outside. Mandela's wife, Winnie, who had become a leading **activist,** had a series of **banning orders** imposed on her, and the police kept a close eye on all her activities. In 1975, Mandela saw his fifteen-year-old daughter, Zindzi, for the first time in twelve years. The meeting was emotional, made worse by a sad piece of news. Bram Fischer, one of the defense lawyers in the Rivonia Trial, had died of cancer. Fischer had been born into a rich **Afrikaner** family, but he had devoted his life to helping the deprived majority within his country.

IGNORING THE BAIT

During these long years of imprisonment, Mandela discovered that his reputation as a symbol of the African struggle was actually growing. The government also realized this, and decided to tempt him into making some **compromises.** They saw that Mandela's **opposition** to the Bantustan policy was an important stumbling block. In 1976, Mandela was visited by Jimmy Kruger, the South African minister of prisons. Kruger offered Mandela his freedom, as long as he agreed to stop working for change and "retire" to Transkei, one of the separate **homelands** for blacks. Mandela refused immediately.

SERIOUS BUSINESS

By 1980, there was a powerful "Free Mandela" campaign launched in South Africa, which attracted widespread support around the world. There were also international sports and cultural **boycotts** of South Africa because of its **apartheid** policies. The South African government felt threatened from all sides, and put more pressure on Mandela to agree to terms. In 1985, Kobie Coetsee, the minister of justice and one of the most important politicians in South Africa, visited Nelson.

Huge concerts and rallies, like this one in London, kept the "Free Mandela" campaign in the international news.

The two men had a series of informal discussions and even became somewhat friendly with each other. However, Mandela remained firm that blacks and whites should not be separated in South Africa, and he insisted that the ANC might still need to use violence if the government did not make changes. Despite these unchanging views, he was willing to listen to Coetsee.

"South Africa belongs to all who live in it, black and white. We do not want to drive you into the sea."
Nelson Mandela, addressing South African government officials in 1988

THE TASTE OF FREEDOM

One of Nelson Mandela's most consistent statements in all his discussions with South African government officials was simple: prisoners cannot enter into contracts. Only free men can **negotiate.** If one man was really the prisoner of the other, then any deal would be meaningless. The government felt pressure to reach an agreement, though. Many foreign companies were leaving South Africa because of **apartheid** and because of the violence that they feared could soon erupt there. The campaign to release Mandela was becoming popular among many white South Africans, and blacks were impatient for change. By 1988, Mandela learned that none other than President P. W. Botha was planning to meet him.

TOP-LEVEL TALKS

This meeting was delayed when President Botha was hospitalized in January 1989. He withdrew from active government, but kept his position as **head of state.** In this role, he still wanted to meet Nelson Mandela. The meeting between Nelson and the man called "die Groot Krokodil" ("the great crocodile") because of his stubborn temper finally took place on July 5, 1989. Although the meeting had a friendly tone, Botha refused Mandela's most important demand—to release all **political prisoners.**

In August 1989, F. W. de Klerk became the new president of South Africa. Two months later, he released Walter Sisulu and seven other famous Robben Island prisoners. They were not given **banning orders,** and were allowed to speak legally as ANC representatives. The new president continued to make improvements by removing many of the restrictions imposed by apartheid. Mandela felt that de Klerk seriously wanted change, and met him on December 13, 1989. Mandela pointed out that even if he were released, he and other ANC leaders making public speeches would have to be rearrested immediately if the ANC remained an illegal organization.

President P. W. Botha could not reach an agreement with Nelson Mandela.

FREE AT LAST

It turned out that President de Klerk had listened to much of what Mandela had said. On February 2, 1990, he addressed the South African Parliament and made several dramatic announcements. He would lift the bans on the ANC and 33 other organizations, he would free all political prisoners who were not convicted of violence, and he would end the death penalty. "The time for negotiation has arrived," he said.

Nelson Mandela raises his fist in triumph as he walks out of prison on February 11, 1990.

A week later, de Klerk invited Mandela to his office and informed him that he would be freed the next day. There was a short debate, because, strangely enough, Mandela felt that the next day was too soon. He needed time to prepare for his release, and another week or so in prison would hardly count after all the years he had spent there. De Klerk, however, pointed out that foreign journalists had been told of the date and that he could not let them down. Mandela finally agreed, and the two men raised their glasses in a toast.

Mandela had been transferred from Robben Island to another prison in 1982, and had spent his last five years in a more comfortable prison in Paarl, near Cape Town. It was through these prison gates that he walked, accompanied by his wife, Winnie, on the afternoon of February 11, 1990. His 10,000 days in prison were over and, at the age of 71, he was preparing to start a new life.

THE NEW SOUTH AFRICA

Most people in South Africa were overjoyed about Nelson Mandela's release. Crowds filled cities and towns in celebration. Cameras followed his every move as he greeted well-wishers at the prison gate and was driven away. The first great reception, a Grand Parade past the Cape Town City Hall, set the tone for many similar expressions of joy and hope in South Africa.

However, Mandela never lost track of his role as a leader. Addressing an emotional gathering of 120,000 people in Soweto, he promised to continue the struggle, but also insisted that all South Africans unite to fight crime in the **townships.** In other speeches, he praised the work of de Klerk, and he persuaded the ANC to prove its commitment to **reconciliation** by abandoning the threat of violence.

On July 5, 1990, Nelson Mandela was elected president of the ANC. In the next few years, he used this role to press for more cooperation among all South Africans. His words were echoed by President de Klerk, who announced that general elections would be held in 1994.

"I am disturbed as many other South Africans no doubt are, by the **spectre** of a South Africa split into two hostile camps— blacks on one side . . . and whites on the other, slaughtering one another."

Nelson Mandela in a memo to President P. W. Botha, January 1989

PRESIDENT MANDELA

Nelson Mandela and F. W. de Klerk were jointly awarded the Nobel Peace Prize several months before South Africa's April 1994 general election.

South Africa's general election in April 1994 was the first in which people of all races could vote. Nelson Mandela led the ANC to victory, helping the party win 252 of the 400 seats in the South African Parliament. Near the end of the campaign, Mandela debated F. W. de Klerk on television. At the end of the debate, which at times was heated, Mandela reached across to shake de Klerk's hand. He told his political opponent that "I am proud to hold your hand for us to go forward."

After becoming president in May 1994, Nelson Mandela tried to strengthen the ties between South

Nelson Mandela proudly—and publicly—casts his vote in his country's first free general election in 1994.

Africans instead of promoting the interests of just one racial group or political party. He helped write a new South African **constitution,** which took effect in February 1997, and which guarantees basic rights to all citizens. At the same time, he approved new laws to improve the quality of health, housing, and education for needy South Africans.

HEAD OF STATE

As president, Nelson Mandela became South Africa's **head of state** and a symbol of his country both at home and abroad. He represented the whole nation, whether in delivering a New Year's message to South Africa's Parliament or in laying the first brick for a new school in Soweto.

Nelson Mandela's visits to foreign cities attracted thousands of well-wishers. These people were cheering not only for the courage and dignity of Mandela the man, but also for the ideals of the new country that he had done so much to shape.

HEALING THE WOUNDS

J ust as important, Mandela tried to change attitudes and to begin a time of healing in his country. One of the most important moves he made was to establish the Truth and **Reconciliation** Commission. This group has heard the **testimony** of those who suffered injustices under the **apartheid** system, and it has offered an **amnesty** for those prepared to appear before it. These people have included many—such as former police officers, soldiers, and government officials—who had once kept apartheid in force.

INTERNAL PROBLEMS

The job of governing South Africa is not an easy one, and Nelson Mandela faced many difficulties from the start. One of his most important concerns was to make sure that the white population did not flee the country in fear that the black **majority** would attack them in revenge for all the past events under apartheid. Mandela included people of all races in his **cabinet**, and made great efforts to show that South Africa is—and

Archbishop Desmond Tutu, chairman of the Truth and Reconciliation Commission, shakes hands with former South African president F. W. de Klerk.

should remain—the mother country to all who live there. His teamwork with F. W. de Klerk had earned them the 1993 Nobel Peace Prize. As president, Mandela tried to enlist the support of de Klerk, who served as deputy president from 1994 to 1996. The cooperation of these two men from such different backgrounds was a symbol of the moves to unite all South Africans.

Young black children arrive in 1996 for their first day at a school that had previously been for whites only.

There was another problem, this time involving other black groups. The Zulu people, who make up a large part of the South African population, had long believed that their territory did not have enough **autonomy.** They continued to make this complaint after the 1994 election, and their main political party, the Inkatha Freedom Party, even abandoned its seats in Parliament because of these disagreements.

The memory of those who died and the prospect of more violence troubled Nelson Mandela during the time he was president.

CONTINUING VIOLENCE

It was not surprising that one of the first issues that Nelson Mandela addressed soon after his release was the problem of violence. Crime has always been a concern in South Africa, and it did not disappear overnight when free elections were held. Under President Mandela, the South African police force had to change its character: instead of enforcing **apartheid,** it had to concentrate on crime. The **majority** in the country can now respect the police, but violence is still a concern for all South Africans.

The role of sports

South Africa is a nation that loves sports, and most citizens follow their national teams, nicknamed the Springboks, with great enthusiasm. During the years of apartheid, there was a sports **boycott** of South Africa—he international community believed that this would put more pressure on the government to change conditions. The boycott was lifted after the 1994 election, so South African teams and individuals could once again compete around the world. South Africa hosted the 1995 World Cup for rugby—a sport usually associated with the **Afrikaner** population in South Africa. The Springboks won the World Cup, but their greatest joy was seeing President Mandela sharing in the celebrations at the stadium.

Passing on the Torch

Nelson Mandela turned 80 years old in July 1998. It was a time for reflection, and he announced that he would be stepping down as president when his term of office ended in 1999. He knew that he was too old to tackle the difficult day-to-day responsibilities of government. He also remembered how he, along with Walter Sisulu, Oliver Tambo, and other young ANC members, had been impatient with the "old" ANC leadership some 50 years before.

Mandela was pleased when the ANC chose a bright, younger politician, Thabo Mbeki, to replace him as ANC leader. Mandela had become a political father figure to Mbeki, who had seen firsthand how the government operated. Mandela gave his full support to the ANC, and to Mbeki, in the 1999 elections. The ANC won these elections easily, and in an emotional moment in May 1999, Mandela stepped down as president and made way for Thabo Mbeki.

Nelson Mandela was the first to congratulate Thabo Mbeki when he became South Africa's new president in May 1999.

MANDELA THE MAN

Nelson Mandela has had to make many sacrifices in his long life. One of the most painful aspects of his being a public figure—and in particular, one who has spent his time either on the run or in prison—is his separation from his family. In some ways, Mandela had an early introduction to such separations with the death of his father and his move to live with the **regent** as a child.

THE MARRIAGE SACRIFICE

Nelson Mandela was still in his mid-twenties when he married Evelyn Mase, a cousin of Walter Sisulu. The couple had four children—two boys and two girls—although one of their daughters died as a child. They struggled to make ends meet, but by the time Mandela started his own legal practice, they had begun to grow apart. Evelyn grew increasingly religious, and came to believe that the ANC was against religion. Nelson, for his part, believed that Evelyn's religious devotion made her more willing to accept the injustices of **apartheid**. The two finally divorced in 1957.

A year later, Mandela married Winnie Madikizela. Winnie was a great support for Nelson, and agreed with his goals within the ANC. Her house in Soweto became a center for ANC **activists** while Nelson was serving his long prison sentence. However, in the late 1980s, Winnie became associated with rough young men who tortured—and in one case, killed—other black people who did not agree with them. Nelson could not support her involvement, and they, too, were divorced.

After his release from prison, Nelson Mandela became friendly with Graça Machel, the widow of the great Mozambique freedom fighter Samora Machel. The two were married in 1998, and have become a popular couple in South Africa.

Mandela receives a standing ovation while addressing the General Assembly of the United Nations.

In 1993, Nelson Mandela visited Robben Island and paused to hammer stones in the same yard where he had done hard labor for almost twenty years.

THE INTERNATIONAL ARENA

Almost as soon as Nelson Mandela was released from prison, he was swamped with invitations to address various groups across the globe. He has received **honorary degrees** from more than 50 international universities and colleges. On an official level, he has visited many countries and met with many political leaders. One of his most famous trips was to the United States in 1990. While there, he received a medal from the U.S. Congress in Washington and addressed the United Nations in New York City. Also in New York, he made a point of attending a rally in the deprived area of Harlem, where many black Americans still live in poverty. When Nelson Mandela received the 1993 Nobel Peace Prize with F. W. de Klerk, he dedicated the prize to all who worked for peace and stood against racism.

THE BIRTHDAY BASHES

It is at home in South Africa where Nelson Mandela's message has had its greatest effect. Despite continuing difficulties in the country, South Africans celebrate Mandela's birthday (July 18) with parties. Mandela invited 1,000 disabled children to his 79th birthday

50

Simple tastes

Perhaps the best reflection of Nelson Mandela's personal side is his daily routine. His strict sense of self-discipline continues to dictate his actions in the same way that it did while he was serving his sentence on Robben Island and in other prisons. He still wakes up at 4:30 A.M., no matter how late he has worked the previous evening. By 5 A.M., he has begun an exercise routine that lasts for at least an hour. At 6:30 A.M., he has a breakfast of plain porridge, fresh fruit, and milk, while reading the newspapers, and then works at least twelve hours.

party in 1997, and the welcome he gave them was as genuine as the welcome he gave the world leaders who celebrated his eightieth birthday.

In 1998, when Nelson Mandela turned 80, South Africa organized a series of concerts entitled "Gift to the Nation." These marked the launch of a year-long series of celebrations honoring Mandela, which continued until his retirement as president. People who attended were amused and cheered by the sight of their elderly president singing and clapping along with rap musicians, rock bands, and symphony orchestras, as well as a range of traditional African musical groups.

As the new **millennium** begins, Nelson Mandela again lives in Qunu, his childhood village. So much has changed since he was last there—and he can be proud that he was responsible for many of those changes.

Nelson Mandela— Timeline

1918	(July 18) (Nelson) Rolihlahla Mandela born in the Transkei village of Mvezo
1934	Attends Clarkebury Boarding Institute
1937	Enrolls at Healdtown, a **missionary** high school
1938–40	Attends University College of Fort Hare
1942	Completes **correspondence course** from the University of South Africa and earns degree
1942	Joins African National Congress (ANC)
1944	Becomes co-founder of African National Congress Youth League (ANCYL) Marries Evelyn Mase
1947	Elected to the **secretaryship** of the ANCYL
1949	Promotes the Program of Action at ANC national conference
1950	Elected to the National Executive Committee (NEC) of the ANC
1952	Elected national volunteer-in-chief of the ANC's Campaign for the Defiance of Unjust Laws Cleared of charges of **inciting** violence Elected to the presidency of ANCYL and becomes a deputy president of the ANC itself Opens law practice in Johannesburg with his friend Oliver Tambo as partner
1957	Divorces Evelyn Charged with **treason** but found not guilty
1958	Marries Winnie Madikizela
1961	Becomes commander-in-chief of Umkhonto we Sizwe, the armed branch of the ANC
1962	Leaves South Africa secretly to tour other African nations and to gain support and military training for the ANC Arrested on his return to South Africa for having left the country illegally, and for inciting a strike Convicted and sentenced to five years in prison

1963	Charged with **sabotage** while in prison after the secret ANC headquarters are discovered
	Faces possible death sentence if convicted
1964	Rivonia Trial ends with a conviction; sentence is life imprisonment
	Sent to Robben Island prison near Cape Town
1976	Meets Jimmy Kruger, South Africa's minister for prisons, but refuses to accept **homeland** policies in return for his freedom
1982	Transferred to prison in Paarl, near Cape Town
1985	Meets Kobie Coetsee, minister of justice
	No agreement, but preparation for future high-level meetings
1989	Meets President P. W. Botha but fails to reach agreement on terms for a release from prison
1989	Meets new president, F. W. de Klerk
1990	(February 11) Released from prison
	(July 5) Elected president of the ANC
1993	Awarded the Nobel Peace Prize with F. W. de Klerk
1994	Elected South Africa's president in country's first election in which all South Africans can vote
1996	Divorces Winnie Mandela
1998	Marries Graça Machel
1999	Retires from active politics at the end of his five-year term as president

GLOSSARY

activist someone who devotes time and energy to a cause

Afrikaner white South African whose ancestors came from the Netherlands

amnesty official pardon

ancestor person in the past who was part of the same family or group

apartheid system of government rules that made whites and blacks live apart from each other in South Africa

appeal legal case aimed at reversing the outcome of a previous case

articled clerk someone who is training to be a lawyer and is gaining work experience in a law firm

autonomy freedom for an area to take care of itself, with little involvement by the country's government

banning order government document that limits where someone can go and what he or she can do

boycott to avoid dealing with a company, service, or even a country in order to force it to change

cabinet closest advisers to a political leader, who help govern a country

civil disobedience protesting against unfair laws by legal means, such as marches and demonstrations

civil war war between two or more groups within a country

clan group of related families

colonial pertaining to countries that are being ruled by other countries

coloreds in South Africa, people of mixed white and black background

communist supporter of a system of government in which property and industry are controlled by the government, and not by individuals

compromise agreement where two sides each give in a little

conservative cautious and unwilling to change things in politics

constitution written document that states how a country or organization will be run

correspondence course course of study completed by mail

defendant someone who is accused of a crime in court

democratic having to do with the right of all people in a country to have a voice in the government

elder older member of a tribe or other social group

establishment the people who own, rule, or write about a country

ethnic having to do with people's nationality or race

expelled forced to leave

grass-roots basic level, as in the widest level of support for a cause

guardian someone with the legal right to act as someone else's parent

guerrilla small-scale warfare, often involving hiding in the countryside to fight larger armies

head of state someone who acts as a leader of a country

homeland place where black South Africans had to live under apartheid

honorary degree award given by a university or college to someone who is well-respected

human rights basic rights that all people should have, no matter where they live

incite to persuade people to do something, such as taking action against a government

militant supporting violent action in order to achieve political goals

missionary promoting a religious view, usually Christian

monotonous boring and unchanging

morale sense of confidence and shared purpose within an organization

negotiation peaceful discussion to solve a dispute

opposition strongly held view against something

parliamentary representation right to elect people to represent a group

petition letter signed by many people asking a government for something

political prisoner prisoner whose crime was committed because of a disagreement with the government

prejudice dislike of a person or group for no good reason

preside to have control over a group

racism belief that one's own race is superior to others

radical favoring extreme solutions to a problem

reconciliation bringing together of opposing groups

regent someone who acts in place of a king or prince

sabotage deliberate destruction of things for a political reason

secretaryship leadership position in an organization

spectre ghostly symbol

state of emergency time when many rights, such as free speech, are withdrawn because a government fears violence

suspended sentence criminal sentence that is spent away from prison but under observation

testify to make a statement in court

testimony actual statement of a person in court

township local area, like a town or city, where blacks had to live under apartheid in South Africa

treason crime of trying to overthrow the government

underground in secret, and usually in hiding from the police or other powers

veld word used by Afrikaners to describe South Africa's fertile plains

vigil long period of time that people spend together to show support for someone or something

warrant document that is used in a court of law

MORE BOOKS TO READ

Kizilos, Peter. *South Africa: In the Midst of Change.* Minneapolis: Lerner Pubishing Group, 1998.

Meisel, Jacqueline D. *South Africa at the Crossroads.* Brookfield, Conn.: Millbrook Press, 1994.

Pratt, Paula B. *The End of Apartheid in South Africa.* San Diego: Lucent Books, 1995.

Strazzabosco, Jeanne M. *Learning about Forgiveness from the Life of Nelson Mandela.* New York: Rosen Publishing Group, Inc., 1996.

INDEX